OTELLO

in Full Score

Giuseppe Verdi

Dover Publications, Inc.
New York

INSTRUMENTATION

3 Flutes [Flauti] (and Piccolo [Ottavino]). 2 Oboes [Oboi].
English Horn [Corno Inglese]. Bagpipes [Cornamuse].*
2 Clarinets [Clarini]. 1 Bass Clarinet [Clarone]. 4 Bassoons [Fagotti].

4 Horns [Corni]. 2 Cornets [Cornette]. 2 Trumpets [Trombe].
4 Trombones [Tromboni].

Timpani. Bass Drum and Cymbals [Gran Cassa e Piatti].
Second Bass Drum [Altra Gran Cassa]. Gong [Tam-tam].

Mandolins [Mandolini].* Guitars [Chitarre].* 2 Harps [Arpe].

First and Second Violins [Violini]. Violas [Viole].
Cellos [Violoncelli]. Double Basses [Contrabbassi].

ON STAGE [Sul Palco]:
Lightning [Lampi e Fulmini]. Thunder [Tuono]. Organ [Organo].
6 Trumpets and 4 Trombones (offstage).

IN THE BALLET:
Snare Drum [Tamburo] on stage. Cannon [Cannone].

*The Bagpipes may be replaced by two Oboes; the Mandolins, by two Harps; the Guitars,
also by two Harps transposing an octave down, etc.*

This Dover edition, first published in 1986, is an unabridged republication of the score first published by G. Ricordi & C., Milan. The original Italian front matter has been newly translated into English for the present edition.

Manufactured in the United States of America
Dover Publications, Inc., 31 East 2nd Street, Mineola, N.Y. 11501

Library of Congress Cataloging in Publication Data

Verdi, Giuseppe, 1813-1901.
  Otello : in full score.

  Opera.
  Libretto by Arrigo Boito, based on the play by Shakespeare.
  Reprint. Originally published: Milan : Ricordi, n.d.
  1. Operas—Scores. I. Boito, Arrigo, 1842-1918. II. Shakespeare, William, 1564-1616. Othello. III. Title.
M1500.V48O8   1986   85-754295
ISBN 0-486-25040-7

OTELLO

Lyric drama in four acts.   Poem by Arrigo Boito.   Music by Giuseppe Verdi.

First performance: Milan, Teatro alla Scala, 5 February 1887.

CHARACTERS

OTELLO, Moor, general of the Venetian armada .... *Tenor*

JAGO, ensign .... *Baritone*

CASSIO, squadron commander .... *Tenor*

RODERIGO, Venetian gentleman .... *Tenor*

LODOVICO, ambassador of the Venetian Republic .... *Bass*

MONTÀNO, Otello's predecessor as governor of the Island of Cyprus ... *Bass*

A HERALD .... *Bass*

DESDEMONA, Otello's wife .... *Soprano*

EMILIA, Jago's wife .... *Mezzo-Soprano*

Soldiers and Sailors of the Venetian Republic
Venetian Ladies and Gentlemen
Cypriot Citizens of both sexes
Greek, Dalmatian and Albanian Men-at-Arms
Children of the island — An Innkeeper
Four inn servants — Rabble

Scene: A coastal town on the Island of Cyprus.
Time: End of the fifteenth century.

CONTENTS

FIRST ACT

OTELLO

ATTO PRIMO

L'esterno del Castello.

Una taverna con pergolato. Gli spaldi nel fondo e il mare. È sera. Lampi, tuoni, uragano.

Allegro agitato. (♩=76.)

Musica di Giuseppe Verdi.

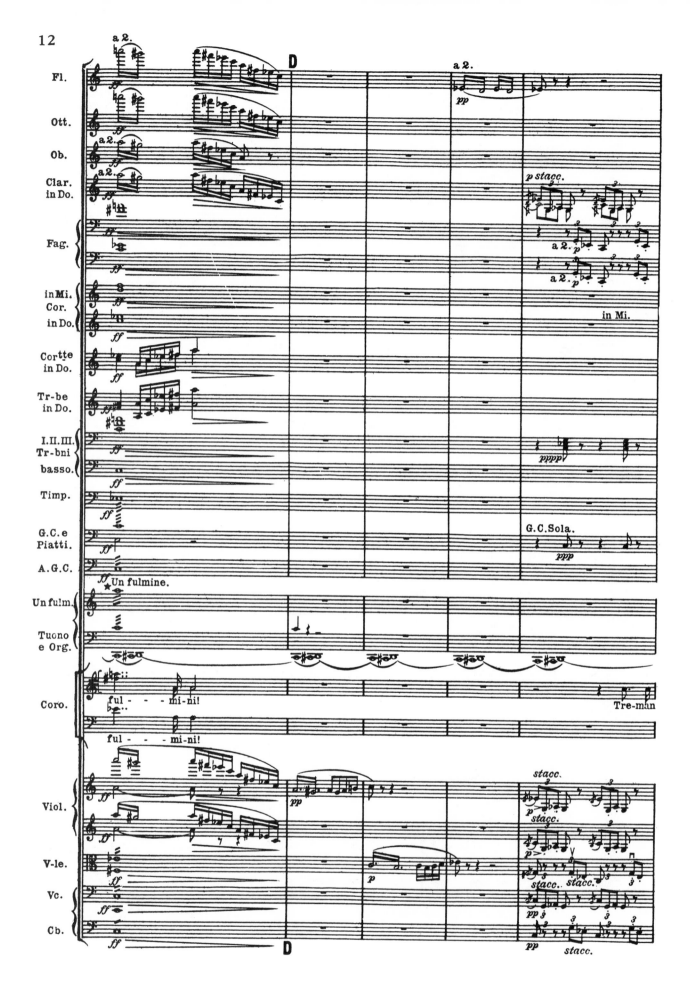

18

(Otello entra nella rôcca, seguito da Cassio, Montano e soldati)

50

Levare qualche registro dell' Organo per far più piano.

54

72

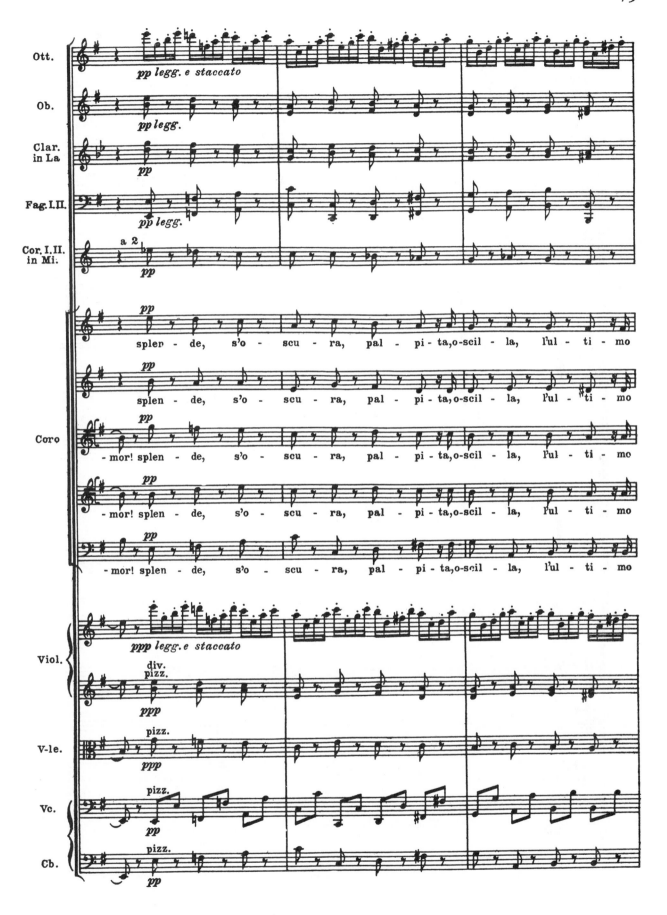

88

stram - bo be - va con me, be - va con me, be - va, be - va,

mon - do pal - pi - ta_____ quand'io son bril - lo! Sfi - -

be - va, be - va,   be - - - - - - va,   be-

119

123

-dan-do: sommossa! sommossa!   Va!   spargi il tu-mul-to, l'or - ror;   le cam-pa-ne ri-suonino a

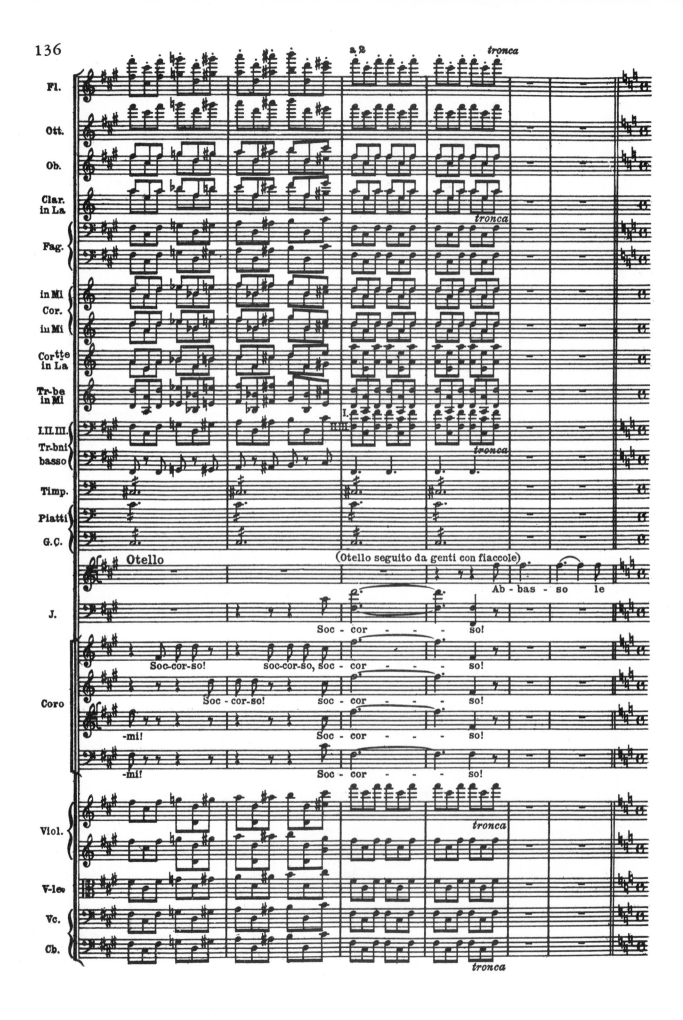

139

(vano di rientrare nel castello.)   (Restano soli Otello e Desdemona.)

fre - - mi -to,   la pugna   e il vol gagliar   - do al - la brec - cia   mor-

156

160

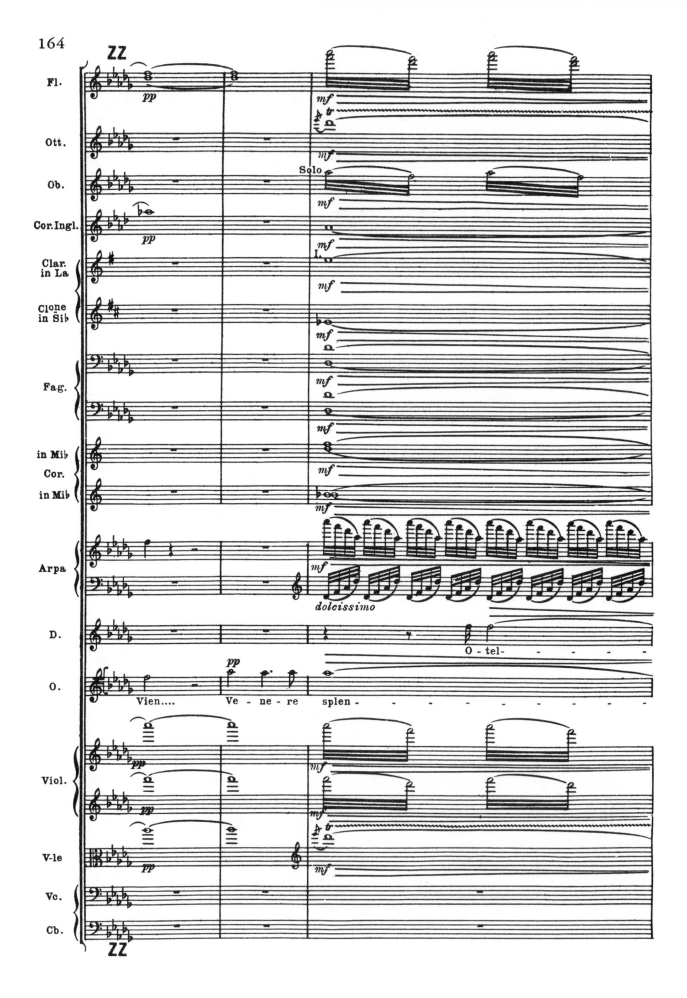

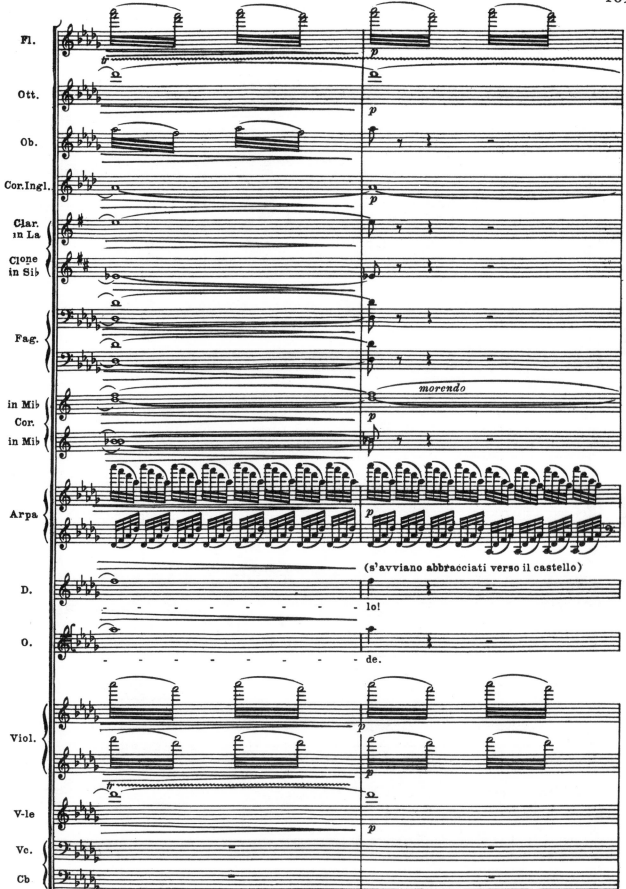

Fine dell' Atto primo.

ATTO SECONDO

Una sala terrena nel Castello.

Una invetriata la divide da un grande giardino. Un verone.

174

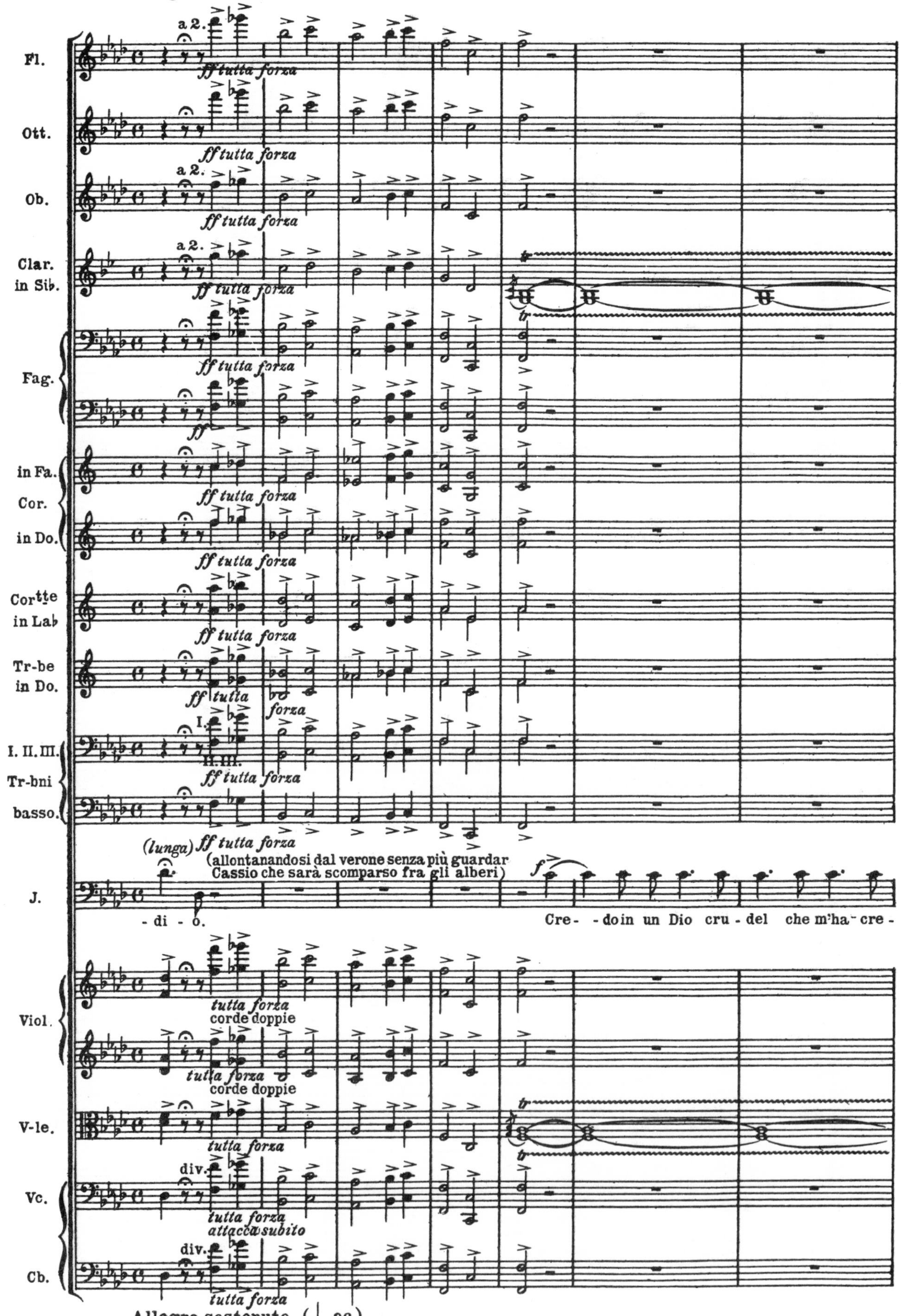

-a-to si-mi-le a sè, e che nel-l'i-ra jo no - - - - -mo.

179

ger - me del-la cul - - la

190

196

202

(Finito il Coro, Desdemona bacia la testa d'alcuni tra i fanciulli, e alcune donne le baciano il lembo della veste, ed essa porge una borsa ai marinai. Il Coro s'allontana. Desdemona, seguita poi

da Emilia, entra nella sala e s'avanza verso Otello.)

228

-lor che in me s'in - fon-de tan-t'è ve - ra - ce che di gra-zia è de - gno.___ In-ter-ce-do per

232

266

269

Ma pur se gui - da è la ragio - ne al ve - ro u - na sì for - te conget - tu - ra ri-

-ser - bo che per po - co al - la cer - tezza vi con - du - ce. U - di - te.

276

279

298

Fine dell' Atto secondo.

ATTO TERZO

La gran sala del Castello.

A destra un vasto peristilio a colonne. Questo peristilio è annesso ad una
sala di minori proporzioni; nel fondo della sala un verone.

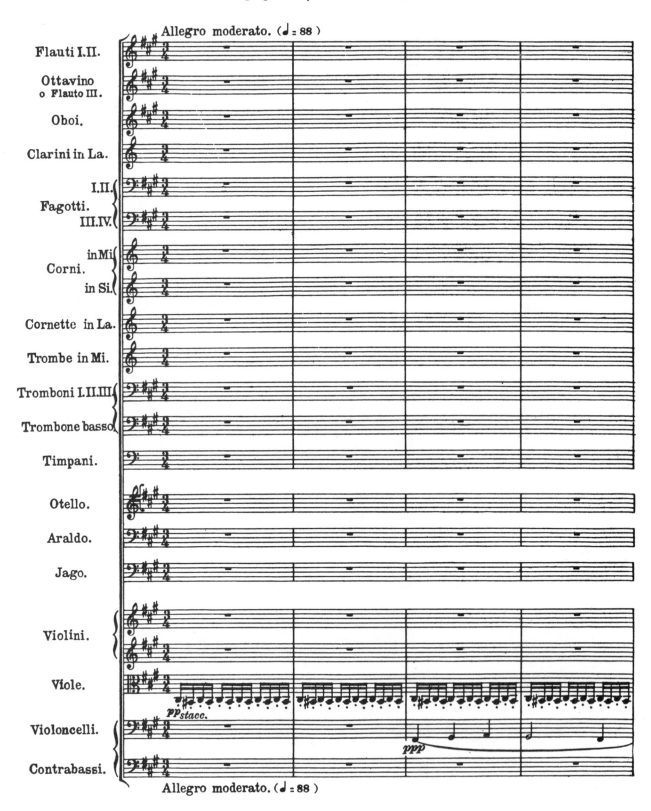

Si alza il sipario.

305

D
Fl.
Clar. I. in La.
Fag. I. II.
D.
-tà.
O.
con eleganza
Ep-pur qui anni-da il de-mo-ne gen-til del mal con-si-glio, che il va-go a-vo-rio al-
Viol.
pp
V-le.
Vc.
D
Fl.
Ob.
Clar. in La.
Fag. I. II.
Cor. I. II. in Mi.
O.
-lu-mi-na del pic-cio-let-to ar-ti-glio.
Mol-le-men-te
Viol.
V-le.
Vc.
Cb.
Solo
espressivo
p
con espressione

I.
Ob.
Clar. in La.
Fag. I.
Gor. I. II. in Mi.
D.
Non l'ho me-co.
O.
No; il faz-zo-let-to vo-glio ch'io ti do-nai. De-sde-mo-na,
Viol.
V-le.
Vc.
Cb.
Solo
F
Fag. I. II.
(cupo)
guai se lo per-di! gua-i!
U-na pos-
pp
ppp

Giu - ra e ti dan-na!

Come prima. (♩ = 72)

-fran-to mi scru - ta... io pre-go il cie - lo per te con questo pian - to, per te con

la - grime che da me spreme il duol, le prime la - gri - me.

Otello

S'or ti scorge il tuo

334

336

338

a tempo

D.: -stia-na... Ah!_____ non son ciò che e-spri-me quel-la pa-ro-la or-

O.: Che?

a tempo

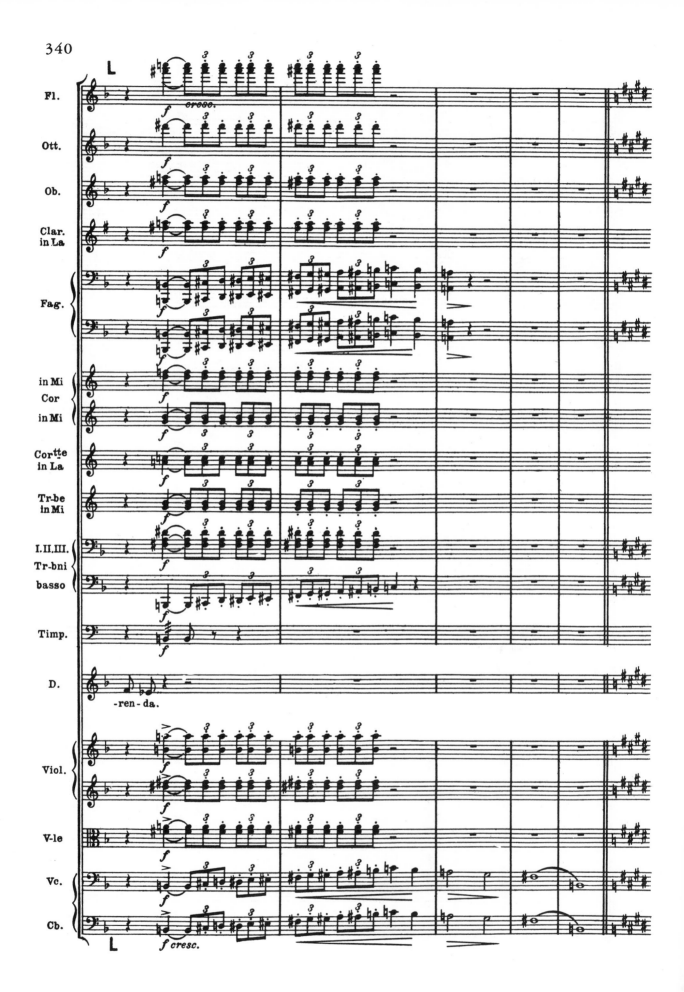

Y
Allegro brillante. (♩.=120)
Timp.
O.
smuo-va.)
(a Cassio indicando il fazzoletto)
J.
Que-sta è una ra - gna do-ve il tuo cuor ca-sca, si la-gna, s'im-pi-glia e
Viol.
pp molto stacc.
V-le
Vc.
Y
Allegro brillante. (♩.=120)
muor. Trop-po l'am-mi-ri, trop-po la guar-di, ba-da ai de-li-ri va-ni e bu-
Clar. in Do
Fag.
pp
I.Solo
-giar-di. Que-sta è una ra-gna do-ve il tuo cuor ca-sca, si la-gna, s'im-pi-glia e

va - go del-l'a-spo e del-l'a - go ___ che in rag - gi tra-mu - ta le fi - - la d'un

382

388

Ved. Appendice (Ballabili) pag. 531

(Entrano Otello, Jago, Lodovico, Roderigo, l'Araldo, Desdemona con Emilia. Dignitari della Repubblica Veneta. Gentiluomini e Dame. Soldati. Trombettieri, poi Cassio)

Vi - va! Ev-vi - va! Vi - va il Le - on di San

Vi - va! Ev-vi - va! Vi - va il Le - on di San

Vi - va! Ev-vi - va! Vi - va il Le - on di San

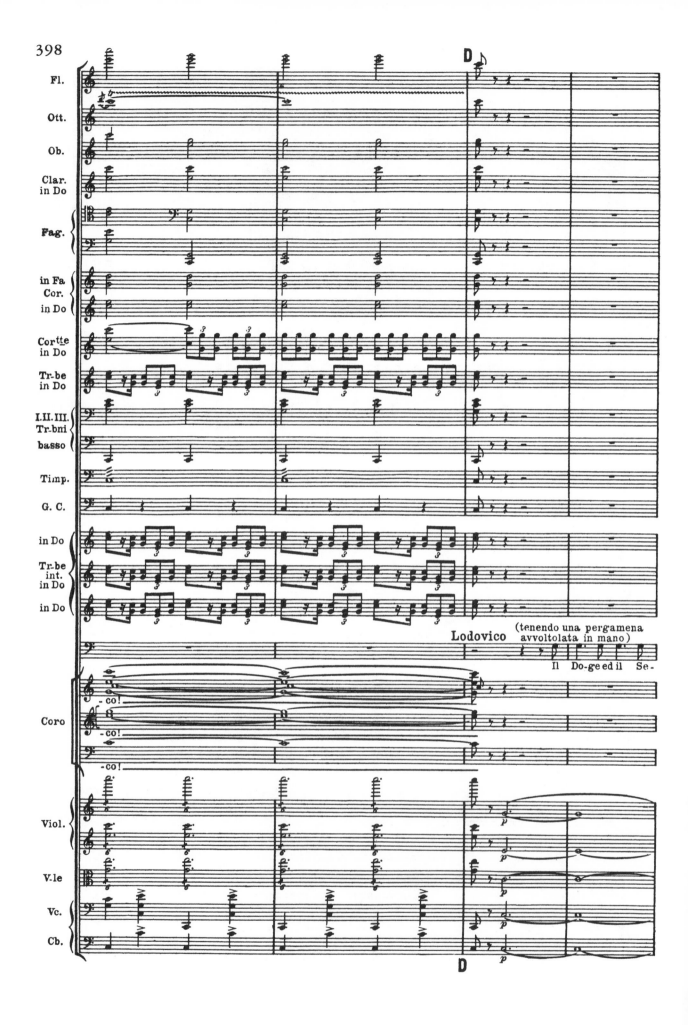

-na-to sa-lu-ta-no l'e-roe tri-on-fa-to-re di Ci - pro.   Io

406

(Emilia e Lodovico sollevano pietosamente Desdemona.)

ria   la spe - - me e il ba - cio   ed or... l'an - go - scia in

-lie - - tail cie-lo e il ma- - re   non   può____sciugar le a-

col canto

ma - re stil - - - le del mio do - lor, lea-ma-re stil-le del mio do-

421

437

447

allargando

allargando

(Restano Otello e Jago soli)

458

Fine dell'Atto terzo.

ATTO QUARTO

La Camera di Desdemona.

Letto, inginocchiatoio, tavolo, specchio, sedie _ Una lampada arde appesa davanti all'immagine della Madonna che sta al disopra dell'inginocchiatoio. _ Porta a destra. Un lume acceso sul tavolo. È notte.

Recitativo.

Clar. in La.

D.

(sedendo macchinalmente davanti allo specchio)

-to. Mia madre a-ve-va u-na po-ve-ra an-cel-la in-na-mo-ra-ta e bel-la; e-ra il suo no-me

Viol.

V-le.

Vc.

Cb.

Recitativo.

D.

Bar-ba-ra; a-ma-va un uom che poi l'ab-ban-do-nò, can-ta-va u-na can-zo-ne: *la canzon del*

Viol.

V-le.

Vc.

Cb.

dolce
C. ingl.
(ad Emilia)
parlante
marcate
D.
Sa-li-ce. =Mi di-scio-gli le chio-me. Io que-sta se - ra ho la me-mo-ria
Viol.
V-le.
Vc.
Cb.
E Andante mosso. (♩ = 84)
Fl.
Ob.
Clar. in La.
I. Solo
III. Solo
Fag.
morendo
pie - na di quel-la can-ti - le - - na:
cresc. e string.
dim. ed allarg.
pp
p
E Andante mosso. (♩ = 84)

(a Emilia, levandosi un anello dal dito)

- sir le ru - pi. " Ri-po-ni quest'a - nel-lo.

Po - ve - ra

Sal - ce! Sal - ce!" **O** Stringendo il tempo. E - milia, ad - di - o.

Come m'ardon le ciglia! È pre - sa-gio di pianto.

506

511

516

MM
Poco meno ma pochissimo.

Niun mi te-ma   se anco armato mi ve - de.   Ec-co la fi-ne del mio cam - min...   Oh!

Fine dell' Opera.

BALLABILI

(composti per la rappresentazione al Teatro dell' Opéra di Parigi il 12 Ottobre 1894)

Fl.
Ott.
Ob.
I.
Clar. in La
I.
in Mi
Cor.
in Mi
Timp. Mi e La
P. Soli
C. e P.
Tamb.
Cb.
2
I. Solo
Solo
pp
2

③ Canzone Araba

Cancone Greca

La Muranese

560

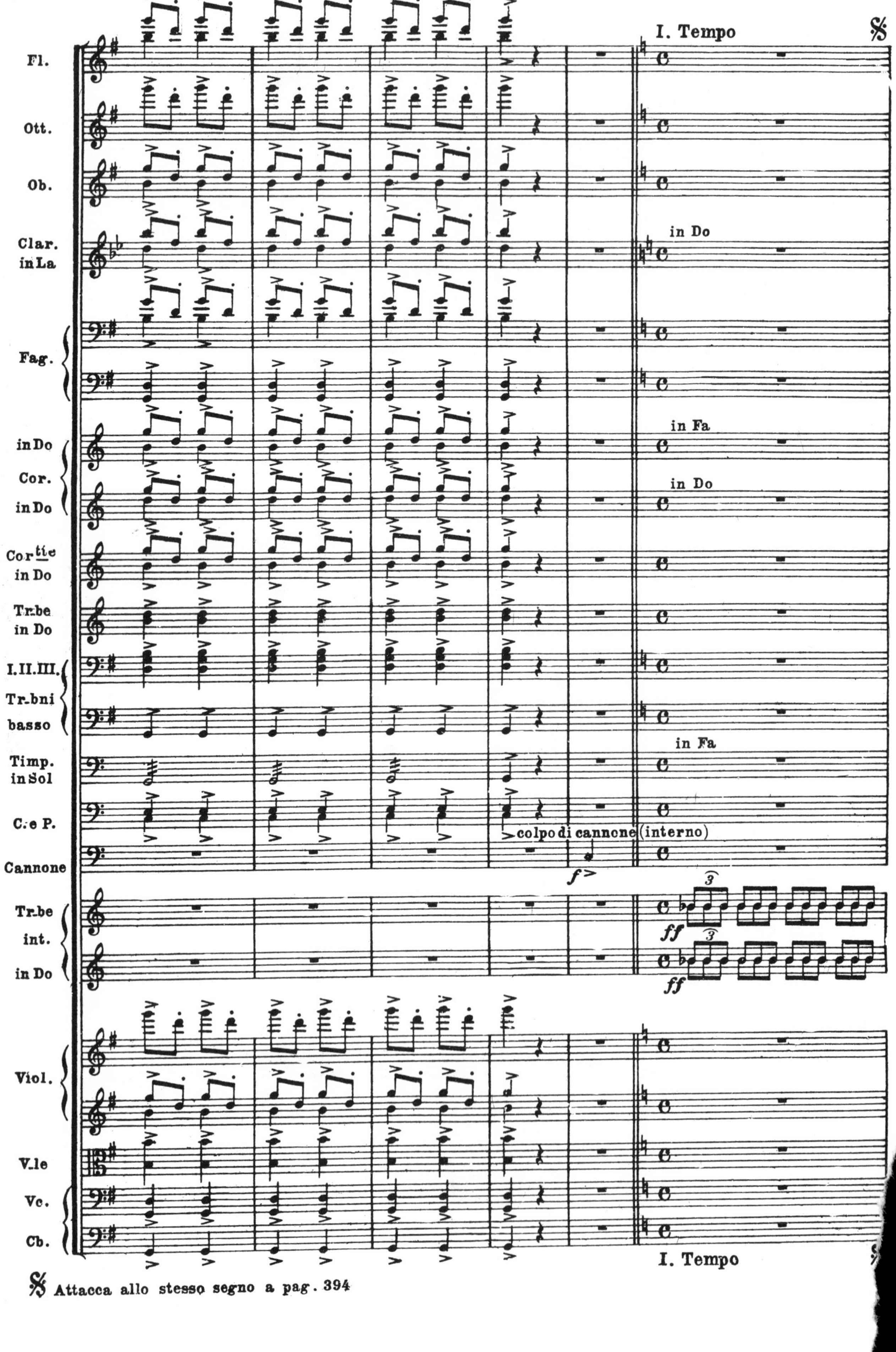

𝄋 Attacca allo stesso segno a pag. 394